LFIG

Labour
Business
.org

Consultation paper: Taxation of the self-employed

Off payroll regulations (freelancing):

The mess we are in and how to get out of it

Philip Ross
freelancing@labourbusiness.org

15th September 2019

Off payroll regulations (freelancing):

The mess we are in and how to get out of it

by Philip Ross

First edition, September 2019

Philip Ross - rosspe@talk21.com

Published at www.Lulu.com and at labourbusiness.org

Thanks to Ajay Nehra for cover design, proof reading and support.
Thanks also to Rebecca Seely-Harris for support and advice.
To Phil McCauley for moral support.
Also to the Labour Business members and Executive.

Contents

Labour Business Consultation

Our Vision for Developing Labour's Business Policies

Founded in 1972, Labour Business is the only business membership group affiliated to the Labour Party. We are independent of the Party, but influential within it.

The purpose of this Action Plan is to set out the framework for an integrated programme of business engagement and policy development by **Labour Business** which will support the development of evidence-based business policies for a future Labour Government.

In approaching our policy development work, we consider it crucial that the business policies we develop are based on evidence collected from stakeholders in the business community, which is why we are inviting key business organisations and trade unions to collaborate with us in a business engagement process over the coming year which will gather the evidence for subsequent policy development.

The **Labour Business Manifesto** that results from this process will be owned and published by **Labour Business;** it will not automatically become Labour Party policy. That said, our aim will be to make a persuasive contribution to the Party's own manifesto for the next general election.

By taking part in this policy development process, partner organisations will not be endorsing any specific Labour Party policies. However, they will help to ensure that the business policies of a future Labour Government are road-tested, evidence-based and realistically achievable.

Vision, Values and Priorities (the "Pediment")

This first section of the **Labour Business Manifesto** will set out an overarching narrative of our vision, values and priorities for the next Labour Government's approach to business, wealth creation and the broader economy.

The overarching narrative will:

- Build upon Stephen Kinnock's pamphlet *"Partners for a New Kind of*

Growth" (published in 2016 by **Labour Business** at http://lfig.org/publications/the-labour-party-and-business-partners-for-a-new-growth/)

- Be anchored in a key statement from Labour's GE2017 Manifesto: "Labour understands that wealth creation is a collective endeavour – between workers, entrepreneurs, investors, and government. Each contributes, and each must share fairly in the rewards." **For the Many not the Few,** at page 8.

Introduction to this consultation paper

This consultation paper comes under the policy area of self-employment and freelancing. One of our mandated areas to consider is taxation for the self-employment. This consultation covers a subset of that, namely IR35 and the taxation of limited company contractors (those who use personal service companies).

The biggest change to our working practices as a result has been in the growth of self-employment. Self-employment takes many forms and is across all sectors of our economy. While Labour is naturally concerned about issues of bogus and forced self-employment it is equally concerned about providing support and encouragement to those who are self-employed.

The number of self-employed has risen from 3.3 million people (12.0% of the labour force) in 2001 to 4.8 million (15.1% of the labour force) in 2019[1]. It is estimated

1

by the CRSE to contribute some £2.71bn annually to the economy.

In 2015 Labour Business published a policy document entitled 'The Freelancing Agenda' which argued that freelancers needed to be taken seriously by policy makers. It put forward a number of recommendations to help freelancers be recognised, protected and nurtured. Labour Business believes that the self-employed need to have their own policy agenda.

That report focused on the entire self-employment spectrum but touched also on the issue of Independent Professionals who did contract work. The report noted the issues around IR35 and the uncertainty and problems that this caused.

Since then Co-operatives(UK) have published their report entitled 'Not Alone – trade union and co-operative solutions for the self-employed' and Matthew Taylor of the RSA was commissioned by Theresa

May to look at the issue in a report entitled 'Good Work' which looked at modern working practises. Though not entirely focused on self-employment it featured highly.

This report though focuses on the issues around IR35. The Taylor report commissioned by the government steered clear of the tax implications for the self-employment and the quagmire of IR35. The Conservative Governments of both Cameron and May have muddied the issues around IR35 even further in a clear demonstration of their lack of understanding of the issues involved.

The current Conservative government has changed the way that IR35 is done by moving both the assessment of and liability for tax from the self-employed person to the engager. It has initially deployed this changed to the Public Sector and at time of writing is finalising the details of deploying this to the Private Sector.

The change sounds subtle but is significant, because if the engager wrongly assesses the freelancer as being self-employed for tax then they themselves become liable for this tax if it is proved otherwise. As could have been predicted risk adverse public sector bodies have been blanket assessing their contingent self-employed suppliers as being employees for tax purpose (though not for employment rights).

Labour Business recognises the value and contribution that freelancers and, in this context, independent professional make to our economy. We want some common-sense proposals which aren't just about squeezing out taxes but are about making self-employment sustainable and prosperous so that it benefits those engaged in the model, the clients that use and our economy as a whole.

Our values for the self-employed are about delivering for the self-employed :

- independence
- self-respect
- personal dignity
- control over their own work and their life

This report aims to build on our previous report – 'The Freelancing Agenda' – and looks at the mess that we are in with IR35 and draws out a set of recommendations some strategic and some tactical that allow to have clear and open debate about tax and the self-employed so we can have a thriving, fair and prosperous economy that is fair to its self-employed workers and benefits from them.

Those who wish to comment on this report are encouraged to email:

freelancing@labourbusiness.org

Background – why Labour Business is interested

Lack of recognition for freelancers

We believe that although freelancers make a distinctive contribution to the economy, there is a common lack of recognition of that contribution in Government and politics. There is a suspicion that the rise of freelancing is an undesirable development. Indeed, freelancers are sometimes portrayed either as people who have been coerced into self-employment, or as people hiding behind a freelancing shell to avoid paying higher and additional taxes, as well as national insurance.

In addition, when the role of freelancers is recognised, it is often misunderstood. Freelancers generate the benefits to business, they are not there as replacements for existing employees, but predominantly through working partnerships with those employees. This symbiotic relationship between employees and freelancers has, however, often been overshadowed by perceptions of their competitive interaction. This common view that freelancers are just a shadow workforce for employees is a misconception.

Freelancers mainly serve a different economic function – particularly in driving innovation and helping firms overcome the challenges faced by risk and uncertainty – and in doing so they help create and sustain employment. There was for a long time very little research on freelancers in this modern economy context. The main reason for this is that their new pivotal role only really come to the fore with the emergence of the innovation-driven economy. The co-author of our previous report – The Freelancing Agenda – Prof Andrew Burke, is now chairman of the think tank the Centre for Research on Self-employment (CRSE) which has been at the forefront of fresh research in this area. This lack of understanding and of definition around freelancing has had real consequences, since those who choose to become freelancers can encounter unnecessary risks, (particularly in relation to fiscal matters), as well as barriers to trade, as a result of their requirements not being recognized and addressed. Freelancing, self-employment whether you choose to call, needs proper recognition as a legitimate and long term business model.

Labour Business wants the next Labour Government to bridge this understanding gap by delivering a policy agenda that recognises and respects the self-employed, nurtures and protects them as defined in the next section.

Concerns of businesses

Firms who engage freelancers do not consider themselves to be hiring temporary employees, but to be engaging a supplier and to be filling a skills gap. Some firms are comfortable engaging self-employed freelancers, in effect treating them as 'workers[i]'. For work that isn't done on the client premises or is of short duration, this isn't an issue. However, larger firms are not comfortable with this risk, especially if the freelancer they are engaging is on a high fee rate. They will usually insist that the freelancer operates through a limited company – just like their other suppliers. This is also true if they are recruited through an agency. The concerns that firms have, even if they are using an agency, is that they will expose themselves to both tax and employment risks. Namely, that they can be liable for unpaid taxes by the freelancers, and the risk that the freelancer can acquire employment rights with them. This is an important issue because it has influenced the market and encouraged the use of limited liability companies by individuals as opposed to them being self-employed. Thus, the resulting operating model and contract terms in the freelance economy are geared towards mitigating these risks from the perspective of the client. Many of these risks are unfounded, but because freelancing is in the shadows there is a large amount of 'fear, uncertainty, and doubt' that shapes this.

Non-agency freelancers: In industries where there has been a large concentration of freelancers, but where the agency model is not present, many freelancers have continued to operate as self-employed without the need to resort to using limited liability companies. This is the case for musicians, film and television crews as much as it is for actors. These groups are strongly represented by established trade unions. This organised representation has meant there are good industry standards reflected in good terms and conditions for their members. These markets have evolved such that some have contracts which give their members 'worker' status backed up in many cases by collectively bargained agreements. The key element to their members is the ability to offset travel expenses and equipment purchases against tax. In other sectors where representation is weaker, there are no standard contracts and there are much weaker terms and conditions for freelancers. There is a good case here for creating a better market in part through enabling better representation and organisation for freelancers. At the same time, the value added provided by freelancers is based on the ability to hire them on a flexible and agile basis, so it is important that these core features are preserved in any move to create industry wide standards or representation.

The issue isn't just about taxation or national insurance but about the ability for freelancers to be able to operate as businesses and claim necessary business expenses. These things can be items such as travel and accommodation, as training and equipment. Without the designation as a legitimate business, freelancers will lose the ability to compete fairly in the workplace against firms who are supplying the same services.

Complicated supply-chain

The supply chain between an end-client and the freelancer doing the work can be long and complicated.

If a freelancer uses their own limited company (some call this a personal service company) the liability for tax falls with the freelancer or more accurately with their limited company. Businesses who engage a freelancer do not have any liability for tax. Often, they engage staff through an agency. In doing so they are looking for a simplified supply chain.

The supply-chains can often be long and complicated. The diagram below is modelled on a real-life contract arrangement (though the names of the firms have been changed). People can be working side by side on a project doing the same or similar work, yet their pathway to doing that project can be very different. (A bit like people staying in a hotel, some may have booked direct others through a travel agent, others via an internet broker and others as part of a holiday charter). All are guests are staying at the hotel, and all are equal, but have booked under different terms.

On a project, some staff on it may be direct employees of the end-client, others may be from a firm directly engaged to do the project. This firm may have sub-contracted to a specialist firm to do some of the work. This specialist firm may supply their own staff but may well have engaged an Agency to find additional skilled staff. The agency finds a freelancer who they engage through their own limited company.

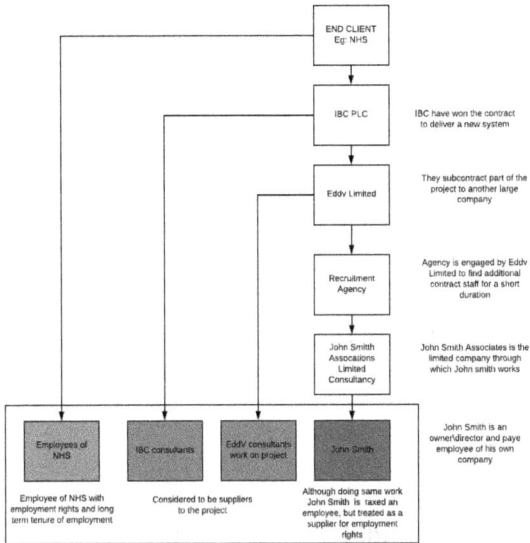

Figure contents (text labels):

END CLIENT
Eg: NHS

IBC PLC — IBC have won the contract to deliver a new system

Eddv Limited — They subcontract part of the project to another large company

Recruitment Agency — Agency is engaged by Eddv Limited to find additional contract staff for a short duration

John Smith Assocaions Limited Consultancy — John Smith Associates is the limited company through which John smith works

John Smith is an owner\director and paye employee of his own company

| Employees of NHS | IBC consultants | EddV consultants work on project | John Smith |

Employee of NHS with employment rights and long term tenure of employment

Considered to be suppliers to the project

Although doing same work John Smith is taxed an employee, but treated as a supplier for employment rights

4 people could be working side by side and doing the same work. The employee of the NHS who has employments rights and tenure of employment. The consultants from the two larger consulancies. They enjoy employment rights via the consultancy, also their expenses are convered as business expenses. (Such as travel and accommodation). Also sick days and holiday John Smith is taxed as a employee, but is treated as a supplier for employment rights. He cannot cover travel or other business expenses. At the end of the project all except John Smith remain as a employees.

The owners of the two consultancy companies can draw a dividend based on the profit made from the work they have done on the project, as unearned income. In part as they employ people and carry a degree of having to pay them even if there is no work after this project. John Smith, although he has taken risk from work on the project and the uncertainty of not having work after the project cannot draw a dividend.

Figure 1- Supply chain

Treatment as employee for tax and as a supplier for employment rights

Currently it is possible for freelancers to be taxed as an employee and have the freedom of operation fiscally as a business withdrawn. Which means no ability to claim business expenses or right to carry income over lean periods or between tax years.

The 2017 Labour Manifesto pledged to 'clamp down on bogus self-employment'. The problem with IR35 is that it is bogus self-employment that is in part driven by HMRC. This is likely to be significantly worse following a further roll-out of the IR35 off-payroll regulations to the private sector.

There is a commitment to align employment rights and tax definitions. Both the CBI and REC (and other groups) feel that it is inappropriate to extend or change the application of IR35 until this has been resolved.

The Government has already said that it will consider the alignment of tax status with employment status. This is welcome and would certainly clarify a number of discrepancies between the two statuses. Meanwhile by rolling out these changes before any realignment is complete, the Government risks exacerbating those problems for clients, agencies and individuals alike. REC, together with many other stakeholders has repeatedly said that Government should refrain from making piecemeal changes to already complicated tax legislation.

(Recruitment and Employment Confederation)

We would expect trade unions to press for case law to establish that it is not possible to tax someone as an employee but deny them rights. A future Labour Government needs to save all parties from a bruising encounter in court by moving to create clarity in this area.

Need for a clear definition of freelancing

We believe that there is a resultant need for a clear definition of freelancing, and recognition of freelancers' positive economic contribution. This would benefit both freelancers and those who use them. This would enable public policy – particularly in relation to fiscal matters, industry, enterprise and the labour market – to help rather than hinder those who choose to freelance and those who engage them.

The freelance market as noted may be wide and deep in varying places, but all are united in the fact that as individuals in business, they have no fixed employer or client.

The important and distinct economic role of freelancers in the modern economy needs to be:

RECOGNISED: Defined as unique economic agents providing an important and distinct economic function to employees and business owners.

PROTECTED: The unique economic value-added provided by freelancers is part of the core of the modern British economy and hence needs to be allowed to thrive.

NURTURED: It is good policy to ensure that British business always has access to a sufficient supply of high quality freelancers in order to optimise the potential of these businesses.

Labour Business recognises that the self-employed work across multiple sectors and in multiple roles across the economy. The 2017 Labour manifesto said it would also introduce "sectoral collective bargaining"

– because the "most effective way to maintain good rights at work is collectively through a union". We think a sectorial approach to self-employment rules could also be appropriate. With a set of standard self-employment rules but variation by sector to take account differing needs and the weight of indicators. For instance, taking into account of the difference between knowledge-based workers and manual workers. Also to stop forced or bogus self-employment being instigated.

History of IR35

The dot com boom, the introduction of the euro, the millennium bug concerns in the late 1990s, all contributed to a huge growth in IT and business projects. Thousands of people switched to working as freelance, the majority of whom sourced work through agencies. Large tax accountant firms sprang up in place of small local accountants to advise this new army of freelancers and to do their accounts. They would propose the most tax efficient model to their clients, which was for contractors to pay themselves a minimum wage and take the rest of their income as dividends, and split these dividends with their spouse and others if they could. The model started to be introduced on an almost industrial scale. It sat firmly on the letter of tax law of what could be done, but away from the spirit of the law that local accountants tended to adhere to, which was that they would be expected to pay a reasonable amount of tax. Naturally, HMRC's predecessor, the Inland

Revenue, was concerned and the response to this in 1999 was the introduction of tax legislation known as IR35. It sought to limit the benefits of using a limited company by taxing the freelancer as an employee. At its heart of this proposition was the belief that most freelancers should be employees of the client, not suppliers. They required that all contracts should be subjected to standard self-employments tests that already existed.

At the time, future Chancellor Philip Hammond MP, contributed to a Hansard recorded debate in 2001 in which he said "one reason why the Government's IR35 initiative has been so damaging and destructive is the fact that it has hit at the most flexible part of the economy."

Impact of IR35

The use of self-employment tests sounds reasonable, except that there was and remains little case law to support knowledge-based workers working on projects. Most case law focused on manual, as opposed to intellectual, labour.

Some of the issues are that these workers don't bring their own tools or arrive in a van. Their skills were specialist and it wasn't easy to provide a substitute if they were unavailable. As they could be augmenting a team (like staff from other consultancies) often they weren't working independently, but co-operatively in a team often under the leadership of a project manager who may also have been a freelancer. The result was that most knowledge-based freelancers were set to fail these tests and be subjected to paying extra tax. When IR35 is applied to a freelancer's earnings it means that they are taxed as an employee (as a Schedule E) and also have to pay their own Employer's National Insurance stamp, an additional 13% of their earnings. This meant that the tax regime for freelancers became considerably worse than that of the self-employed (Schedule D) workers, since Schedule D workers don't pay Employer National Insurance contribution but there was no going back to that model either because of Section 44[2] or client

---

[2] Section 44 of Agency legislation distinguishes temporary workers from professional contractors by use of a limited company. LTD company contractors don't have agency

expectations. The outcome is that these freelancers are taxed as employees but are treated as suppliers for employment purposes. Many new agency freelancers entering the market instead of setting up a limited liability company have instead signed up with umbrella companies. Once these umbrella schemes offered as a service the convenience of not having to maintain a company, do accounts or payroll to freelancers today, many advertise the fact that they are more tax efficient. (Umbrella firms manage contracts both inside and outside of IR35).

Unexpected consequences

Some of the unexpected consequences have been a growth of tax avoidance schemes to work round the provisions of the legislation. The consequences have been the growth of umbrella and payroll firms which has indirectly led to a growth in bogus and forced self employment. Though this is often focus on particular industry sectors as opposed to strictly across the board.

worker rights.m

The last Labour manifesto pledged to abolish umbrella companies. We think that Umbrella firms do have a positive role to play in our economy. They aren't the cause of bogus self-employment but can be symptom of it.

Various other tax avoidance schemes were set up such as Management Service Companies (or composite companies) which Gordon Brown had to outlaw in 2007[ii] . More recently there have been Parliamentary debates and campaigns against Government plans to tax retrospectively who Employee Benefits Trusts to take loans which were later written off to avoid tax. We don't intend to debate these schemes other than that they are a symptom of mess that IR35 has caused.

Conservative Changes to IR35: Changes to IR35 liability

Limitation on dividends

Interestingly George Osborne when he was Chancellor, was rumoured to have considered one of the previous recommendations of Labour Business - the Freelancing Limited company proposition and it was reviewed by the Office of Tax simplification. IPSE the Trade Body for the self-employed engaged Ernest and Young to work up the idea too[iii].

However, his 2015 budget instead replaced dividend tax-credits with a tax-free allowance of £5,000 for everyone with dividends[iv]. This would have an effect on those effectively paying out all their income as dividends making it less tax efficient. Philip Hammond subsequently reduced this allowance to £2,000.

Osborne also suggested that IR35 wasn't working as expected and there were concerns that tax abuses were prevalent in the Public Sector. An automated tool was put into development originally known as an Employment Status Indicator (ESI) but later rebadge or rewritten and became known as CEST[3]. The tool takes a number of case judgements on self-employment and writes them into a logic engine to determine employment tax status. Naturally, HMRC have only selected the cases that are sympathetic to its arguments into the tool. (Unfortunately for HMRC the source code was published as OPEN-SOURCE and was dissected by campaigners who were able to discredit the tool and point the omission of various key arguments , in particular the issue of Mutuality of Obligation).

---

[3] Interesting the tool was built by IT contractors whom HMRC hired for the job. They were assessed as outside IR35 but when applying the tool found themselves caught. 18 of the developers quit HMRC en-mass.

https://www.contractoruk.com/news/0012968hmrc_puts_its_own_it_contractors_inside_IR35.html

In February 2018, Freedom of Information request by website ContractorCalculator request revealed that HMRC's Check Employment Status for Tax (CEST) tool had undergone no formal testing or even informal assessment since its release two years earlier. ContractorCalculator CEO, Dave Chaplin, said: "Given that HMRC has imposed CEST upon the public sector, cheating many honest taxpayers out of thousands in the process, it's astonishing that it has still produced nothing to prove that the tool works, or to hold itself to account."

According to tests by ContractorCalculator, the CEST tool returns a flawed assessment 42% of the time.

It has been argued too that if the CEST tool was applied to work being done by other suppliers (such as the Big 4 consultancies) then it is unlikely that they would pass the test.

The Recruitment and Employment Confederation note:

HMRC have lost a number of high-profile IR35 cases recently. Though these cases predate CEST, presumably the rationale for challenging the intermediary in those cases was used in the design of CEST. If this is the case, then having lost those cases, the rationale for CEST must be wrong so how can parties be confident in CEST results?

Labour Business believes that use of this tool has business and economic consequences and it is not just about tax. The case law that is used in the tool needs to be open and transparent as does the code that is used to generate it. We believe too that there should be no reason why other tools could not be licensed. The use of a single tool to assess all workers for self-employment regardless of the sector or role that they are in, appears to us to be flawed. The use of a tool as a guideline has merits, but the feedback from the public sector roll-out of IR35 is that it created a tragi-comic version of the 'computer says no'.

Roll out to the Public Sector

The Conservative Government rolled out a scheme which changed how tax status was assessed. Instead of the contractor carrying out their own risk assessment and determining their tax status (and in doing so carry the risk and liability for it), the assessment would shift to the engager (the agency or end-client). The engager was instructed to use the CEST tool to determine status and that HMRC would stand by the result offered by the (discredited) tool.

Instead of applying the rules to the entire workforce it limited the changes to be applied only to the Public Sector. At the time HMRC said there were no plans to roll the scheme out to the Private Sector, though unsurprisingly such plans did materialise.

Many contractors have complained that they have funnelled into using a prescribed Umbrella company for their fees and are still asked to sign waivers dismissing their employment or agency worker rights.

Lessons from the roll out

As expected, Public Sector institutions were ill equipped to understand the proposals and tended to use the CEST tool to assess contractors. Often once one single contractor was assessed they then applied the same blanked ruling to all contractors, instead of recognising that different workers may be engaged on different terms and doing different work with varying degrees of control and independence. Authorities tended to be risk adverse and generally assigned all contractors as caught by IR35.

According to REC, it has also damaged the market by undermining the role was smaller agencies to operate within it.

Feedback from small agencies is that they have been removed from the supply chain by larger managed service providers/ vendors/ recruitment process outsourcers because the larger organisations do not trust them to properly manage their obligations. In the public sector this has undermined the Government's plans to improve access to public sector procurement for SMEs.

REC also note that is has damaged the ability to contribute to pensions by some workers:

We understand that prior to the off-payroll reforms in the public sector many off-

payroll workers would have made pensions contributions through the intermediary. We also understand that they have lost this ability as a result of those reforms

The other point they note is:

The research carried out by IFF Research for HMRC in 2017 only contained preliminary figures for off-payroll anti-avoidance in the private sector and the cost for business. There was also no transparency as to how these figures had been calculated, however these figures have driven much of the debate on off-payroll working in the private sector. The research was also limited in that IFF only consulted with public sector clients - they did not consult with the REC, agencies or off-payroll workers. With such drastic changes proposed to the IR35 rules in the private sector, HMRC must conduct a thorough evaluation of (a) the real costs of implementation and (b) the true level of anti-avoidance before introducing any further reforms.

The CBI are concerned about a roll-out to the private sector of these same reforms. In their response to the new proposals they said two things

> *i) Undertake a complete and comprehensive post-implementation review of the public-sector changes.*

The Government has a unique opportunity to comprehensively review the impact the recent reforms have had on the public sector prior to private sector implementation. The evidence presented to date has been limited in scope as has the period of time reviewed. A comprehensive review should be undertaken over at least a full tax cycle since implementation. This should allow issues that occur throughout the tax cycle to be identified, with solutions to tackle issues prior to potential implementation of any private sector changes.

> *ii) Undertake an implementation impact assessment for the private sector.*

Key statistics, such as the total off-payroll anti-avoidance in the private sector and the cost of implementation for business, are driving the debate. However, these figures are preliminary.

With such drastic changes proposed to off-payroll in the private sector, with the full extent of the impact unknown, it is necessary to understand the full extent of costs and an accurate reflection of the true level of anti-avoidance it is aiming to prevent.

NHS

Self-employed nurses and locum doctors were initial victims of the change. Also elsewhere when services like Dermatology services[v] in Nottingham, which were outsourced, existing staff were told that they have to TUPE across to the new provider, anyone trying to work freelance instead was told that their role was caught by IR35 and they would instead have to be paid via a payroll or umbrella company. The very ones that the 2017 Labour manifesto pledged to get rid of.

The blanket approach resulted in considerable anxiety from locum doctors and nurses, who applied for a judicial review. The result was that they obtained a major victory against NHS Improvement under the threat of a judicial review. The IHPA said that "Jim Mackie, the erstwhile head of NHS Improvement, had purported to direct that NHS locum workers were all inside IR35 regardless of their personal circumstances. NHS Improvement accepted our principal argument, namely that any such blanket approach was unlawful because it failed to allow an assessment of each contract. NHS Improvement issued guidance directing trusts to assess each contract on its own basis".

One symptom of the change was that it no longer viable for some nurses to be self-employed especially if they worked in different location. This was because they would be classified as employees not as self-employed and therefore, they couldn't offset overnight accommodation or travel costs against tax. Working in different locations became unviable. The result? Shortage in staff and possible rises in pay rates to get people.

Network Rail

In another case Network Rail has deemed 99% of its contract staff as being caught by IR35.

http://www.itcontractor.com/network-rail-contractors-99-now-caught-by-IR35-off-payroll-rules/

Said Andy Chamberlain of Contractors Group IPSE:-

"Network Rail's assessment that 99% of Network Rail contractors are caught by the off-payroll rules is deeply concerning. These people will now have to pay tax like employees – without any of the rights.

"The preposterously high ratio raises serious questions about how the assessments have been made. Network Rail has openly admitted roles were grouped together and blanket assessed, which undermines Treasury claims that this has not happened."

The rail chaos that resulted from the failed implementation of a new timetable in the summer of 2018 – which led to up to 800 services being cancelled a day   it is believed was linked to IR35. The enquiry into the chaos pointed the blame at Network Rail and their delay in publishing complex new timetables so the train operating companies could prepare for them. Timetabling is a complex task and experts tend to be freelance and have the choice of working with Network Rail (in the public sector) or for Train Operating Companies (TOCs) (who are in the private sector) and helping them to analyse and prepare bids for new franchises. The IR35 blanket assessments is alleged to have caused the shortage of experts as they worked for the TOCs rather than Network Rail.

TFL - London Underground

In the quasi-public sector TFL, it appears, decided it was too tricky to look at individual contracts and decided that *all* contract staff would have to work through an umbrella company. They told staff to take it or leave. Unfortunately for them, many chose to 'leave it' and in months later TFL blamed project delays on IR35 (that too many people left).

Planned roll out to the Private Sector

At the time of writing the new rules have not yet been implemented in the private sector, though they are scheduled to go-live in April 2020. Almost all the trade bodies (CBI, REC, IPSE...) have indicated that this implementation is far too rushed.

This was despite HMRC and Ministers having insisted that there were no plans to roll out the scheme to the Private Sector. A consultation was carried out and to be fair HMRC listen attentively and asked some good questions, but seemingly these responses didn't really help to shape their final recommendations.

Also, they began the consultation by explicitly refusing to discuss Labour Business's concept of a Freelancing Limited Company.

Freelancer Limited Company

6.32. The suggestion was to create a new corporate structure that offers simplified tax treatment, limited liability, a restriction on the frequency of dividend payments, and a requirement for the worker to be paid a minimum salary.

6.33. This is out of scope as it would effectively create a new tax regime, rather than improving compliance with the current rules.

Figure 2- From HMRC consultation document

The concerns raised about blanket assessments for the Public Sector had been raised during the consultation, the recommendations that came from HMRC failed to allay these fears. Indeed HMRC seemed to prefer the concept of blanket assessment as it stated in its consultation:-

"The fragmentation of responsibilities within the labour supply chain results in lengthy, complicated enquiry processes. For example, in many supply chains, different parties have the responsibility for how the work is carried out, how work is supplied, and for ensuring the correct tax is paid, meaning HMRC has to interact with multiple parties within the supply chain".

In other words, HMRC consider the current arrangement as too difficult to police. Also, cases that they have pursued and have been challenged in court have more often than not resulted in defeat for HMRC. This has been a story of the last 18 years. HMRC have been reluctant to bring new cases because of the risk that they could lose and create new and unfortunate precedents in case law. The new IR35 represents efforts to move the metaphorical goal posts.

As a response to the impending changes, in May 2019, HSBC announced that it will cease engaging limited company contractors from this September, saving itself the job of having to assess them under a new IR35 from April 2020.

According to ContractCalculator news site, the bank has told all limited company contractors at key units like HSBC Digital that after one further contract extension, they must choose between being terminated or becoming employees.

It was reported that HSBC has sweetened its ultimatum for some contractors on a so-called 'keep' list it has drawn up, by saying they can stay on as long as they work via a third-party from September. The thinking at HSBC is that it will remove itself from April 2020's obligation to decide contractors' IR35 status, by making them staff or a third-party's PSC. Or just by axing them. However according to legal experts this in unlikely to work.

Also there have been reports of larger consultancies urging contractors to abandon their independent status and to join them instead. Larger consultancies will of course charge larger fees for their work than the independents do. Costs will rise but as profits will be collected by the shareowners of the consultancy firms, it is unlikely that tax take will increase in the long term.

(NB: For the public sector IR35 roll-out there are unsubstantiated rumours that groups like the DWP and even some HMRC projects did exclude some of their workers from the provisions of the legislation).

IR35 Forum and HMRC Accountability

David Cameron's government established what is known as the IR35 Forum which is a roundtable of industry group meeting with HMRC to monitor the problems with IR35. The reforms to IR35 did not come from this Forum and when the meeting took place opposition concerns about the reforms were not recorded in the minutes which led to complaints by forum members, eventually an amendment was made to the minutes, but only after the original minutes had been published which gave a rosy and consensual view of IR35..

Labour Business believe that an IR35 Forum is a good idea, but it needs to be more independent of Government or HMRC control but, should retain its official status. The fact that in the past there were attempts to not minute criticisms and concerns is of great concern. We would recommend an independent chair of this Forum and extend its remit if we are to properly reform IR35. On a wider scale we think that a Minister for HMRC, rather than a Treasury Minister with some responsibility, should be appointed either explicitly or as a defined responsibility so that the actions of HMRC can be held to account in Parliament and via a Select Committee.

Tax and Employee rights

The current situation with IR35 is that freelancers can be taxed as employee but have no employment rights. The roll out of IR35 to the private sector will push this status onto more and more workers. Clamping down on bogus self-employment is something government should do, it should not be creating a market for it.

To be fair government has talked about aligning tax and employment status, but this has yet to happen. We agree with the CBI and others that pushing ahead with these tax changes before resolving the issues around employment status are foolhardy at best.

The Labour movement should work to ensure that anyone taxed as an employee has comparable rights of an employee. Without a doubt this is the trajectory that the economy is currently on.

But in the long term damaging our flexible market for freelancer – particularly in the professional sectors – will not help the economy, we doubt that it will result in an increase in tax. But it will make the proposition of being self-employed to workers less than appealing. The economy will lose its flexibility, overall our productivity would reduce further, and workers would lose the freedom that comes with self-employment. Importantly, we would also be snuffing out any entrepreneurial spirit.

There is an anomaly with IR35 that it is not
the fee that is charged to the end-client that
is subject to the tax, but the fee charged by
the freelancer. Consider the supply chain
example in Figure 1. The end-client, in the
case of our example is the NHS. They are
charged £800 \ day for a consultant to work
on their project. The work is passed down
the supply chain until it reaches 'John
Smith' who does the actual work. On each
stage as it is passed down a slice\margin of
20% is taken from the work. This is not
unusual. Indeed about 50% of the fee paid
by the NHS has gone to middle-men.

If the role is deemed to be inside IR35, then
tax and national insurance need to be
applied, but it is only applied to the fee
payable to John Smith (the £409). Everyone
else is considered to have legitimately
profited from the work that is being done.

	Fee Received	Fee retained	% Retained
IBC	£800.00	£160.00	20
EDDV	£640.00	£128.00	20
Agent	£512.00	£102.40	20
J Smith	£409.60	£409.60	

FEE RETAINED

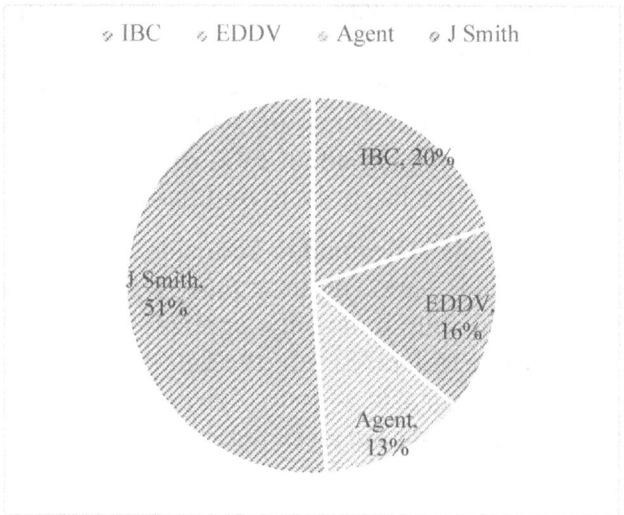

Our concerns: Loss of independence and right to compete for business

> *As Labour Business we believe that one of the big issues behind IR35 is that a professional can work for a consultancy or another firm and be sent in to do a role for a client as a supplier and this is considered to be legitimate business. However, application of the IR35 rules as planned would prevent someone doing the same roles as an independent contractor which is absurd.*

We noted this earlier that a freelancer can be treated as an employee for tax but as a supplier for employment rights. Also, the country risks losing its workforce of flexible independent professional workers. In the short-term fees may rise to compensate for roles being caught by IR35 but in the longer term this differential will disappear as self-employment model would appear less and less sustainable in comparison to secure permanent work.

There is also significant concern about the application of IR35 into the private sector. Industry groups are worried about the shift of liability for from the contractor to either an agency or the end-client. Who the end-client is in a complicated supply-chain arrangement can be difficult to say, especially for project work.

Fiddling with how IR35 is being implemented is not the answer. In the 2017 Manifesto Labour noted and pledged that

"Labour recognises that the law often struggles to keep up with the ever-changing new forms of employment and work, so we will set up a dedicated commission to modernise the law around employment status. New statutory definitions of employment status would reduce the need for litigation and improve compliance. The commission will be led by legal and academic experts with representation from industry and trade unions".

Issues that need to be addressed

The following Principles are taken from the Freelancers' charter that was published as part of our report in 2015. We have scored the new IR35 against these principles.

Principle	Our concern
Freelancers have the right to be issued a contract for the work they are doing or otherwise assume a default basic contract. They have the right to be paid and be paid on time for the services they provide.	Freelancers need either a clear business-to-business contract or a contract as a worker or employee.
Freelancers should be able to compete for work and not be subject to restraint of	Firms will be anxious about engaging freelancers because of IR35 and the risks of

trade by any organisation or association as a result of not having employee or larger company status. Such that clients should not discriminate against, or shy away from freelancers because of concerns over tax and employment status.	tax and the legal complications around it.
Freelancers have the right to a clear definition of their status for both tax and employment purposes.	The new IR35 is by engagement not on the business as a whole. The costs of maintaining a company are being eroded. Contractors will be taxed as employees but with no employment rights.
Freelancers who compete against larger firms for business have the right to be treated as a supplier. If their	This is the fundamental issue with the new IR35 is that it treats independent contractor suppliers

status is assessed for tax or employment purposes then they should have the right to be compared with these others suppliers, not just against employees.	differently from larger suppliers. It is anti-competitive.
Freelancers should not have to pay tax in advance against monies they have not yet earned.	
Freelancer Workers should have the right and ability to pay some additional tax in order to opt-in to register for social welfare support and benefits between contracts. They should have the ability to move to welfare and back again without difficulty.	
Freelancers should have the same	

professional responsibilities as an employee to uphold ethical standards.	
The drivers for freelancing should be professional, economic, and business drivers, rather than ones of tax efficiency. This should apply to both freelancers and those that use them.	With IR35 HMRC seems to assume that the driver for freelancing is tax driven. IR35 makes tax a negative driver for freelancing.
Freelancers have the right to be in business on their own account. Freelancers do not need to employ anyone else, have concurrent clients, or be able to supply a substitute, provide their own equipment, have a distinct work address, or even grow their businesses, to prove their status as a	We think the new IR35 proposals undermine this principle

freelancer.	
Freelancers have the choice to establish a limited liability company dedicated to serve their needs in the marketplace and can use it to carry out both freelancing and traditional small business activities.	It may not be sustainable or viable to maintain a limited company and the opportunities for growth that it offers. Freelance staff needing limited company status will be forced to use umbrella and payroll companies.

Recommendations for next Labour Government

From our consultations and research, we conclude that:

- Implementation of IR35 was not as successful in the public sector as HMRC suggest
- The private sector is not ready for an April 2020 implementation
- Issues of liability for taxes are not clear, clients do not want the liability and neither do Agencies.
- Supply-lines of labour are far more complicated than envisaged by HMRC
- Changes to IR35 will impact more than tax, they impact prosperity and flexibility in the economy
- Changes to IR35 suggest that some supplier roles cannot be done by an independent worker, but only by someone from a third-party consultancy

- HMRC needs to be more accountable and transparent

We recognise:

- the issues of compliance and the need to collect taxes from the self-employed
- that much of the problems are with freelancers using a limited company
- there is not enough case law around self-employment and it is certainly not keeping up with changes to the employment and business market
- that employment rights and tax status need to be aligned

Recommendations :

We think that self-employment and the use of PSCs needs to be considered on sectorial basis as well as across the whole economy. Self-employment and its use is segmented as studies have shown and policies on self-employment and IR35 need to reflect this too.

We propose:

I. Introduce a new business model for freelancers: Freelancers' Limited

Company (FLC) and amend guidance on IR35 to take into account its use

II. Revise guidelines on key tenets of self-employment by industry sector; such as substitution, MOO and others.

III. License use of a FLC by industry sectors allowing third parties like Trade Unions and Trade Association to be accrediting organisations

IV. Define a 4-year window for review of Freelancing policy and use of the FLC. Review effectiveness around the issues of tax revenue; flexibility and prosperity add employment rights. To be considered on sectorial basis.

V. Make HMRC a Ministerial department and formally appoint a Minister for HMRC

VI. Suspend new IR35 roll-out to private and public sector, keep liability with the freelancer. Only move forward when considering results of Taylor review.

VII. Retain the IR35 forum, but with an independent chair

VIII.   Revise the CEST tool for establishing employment status by sector. CEST tool to use agreed precedents and cases and rules. To be agreed by the IR35 Forum as a governing body.

  IX.   Review role of Umbrella and payroll companies for employment rights and tax purposes and as vehicles that create bogus or forced self-employment. Also encourage use of co-operative models.

Recommendations in Detail

- **Recommendation: Consult on the implementation of a Freelancers' Limited Company model**

Do: Introduce a new business model for freelancers: Freelancers' Limited Company (FLC) and amend guidance on IR35 to take into account its use. The original idea did come from Labour Business but has been worked further by IPSE and others.

We think that self-employment is important and needs a modern structure to support it, to encourage, support and protect workers.

Such a reform would show great leadership, vision and ambition for the self-employed in the UK and create a foundation onto which future policies could be built.

So that: We have a fair and tax efficient vehicle for self-employed workers that it fit for the modern economy

Why: The current non-incorporated self-employed model does work for many workers in many sectors. Instead of damaging our economy by moving IR35

liability around, we can keep a simplified model and at same time stop tax avoidance.

How: Run a joint BEIS\HMRC consultation on using such a model. The model will be based around the structure of a Community Interest Company (CIC) and will interface with the guidance on tax and employment right. (See below for use in different sectors)

- Recommendation: Revise guidelines on key tenets of self-employment by industry sector; such as substitution, MOO and others.

Do: When consulting on a FLC consult also on the value of some of the key tenets of self-employment by industry sector. Also ensure that risk of work and loss of work is clearly appreciated in the model.

So that: Tests for self-employment are up-to date reflect those of different sectors and of the knowledge economy.

Why: For some sectors some of the tenets of self-employment make sense, but for others they don't. for some professionals it makes sense that people bring and use their own tools, but knowledge-based workers using a secure client network are unable to do this. Substitution is another, for some roles it should be easy to substitute one for another, but for skilled work the contractor's company may have been hired because they have that unique skill which is built on in-depth knowledge of a technique and possibly a company process. It is not viable to substitute in a person.

This is why we favour a sectoral approach to some of these rules and Labour should consult on what these differing sectors should be.

How: When consulting on a FLC consult also on the value of some of the key tenets of self- employment by industry sector. As a result change guidance materials or embed in legislation. Such changes should be reflected in any automated tool like CEST.

- **Recommendation: License of use of a FLC by industry sectors allowing third parties like Trade Unions and Trade Association to be accrediting organisations**

Why: Different sectors use their self-employed workers differently and under different terms. There is a need to guard against a FLC being used to push through bogus or forced self employment on vulnerable workers. There are leading representative organisations who are experts in their fields, these can be trade associations or trade unions. They could undertake a licensing role for use the FLC for their sectors.

So that: We have a mechanism in place to stop unscrupulous employers and others from using such models for forced or bogus employment schemes.

How: Initially consult and then create a licensing body for the FLC. At present there is a commissioner for Community Interest Companies. Similar would be set up for FLC, the commissioner for FLC would determine the compliance needed and empower groups to act as licensing bodies. We would recommend that licensing bodies should be representative bodies rather then commercial enterprises.

- Recommendation: Make HMRC a Ministerial Department with an appointed a Minister for HMRC / Create a Ministry of Tax

Do: Appoint a Minister for HMRC, or even one for personal tax and one for company taxation.

Why: HMRC's status as a non-ministerial department is intended to ensure that the administration of the tax system is fair and impartial. However, we think this is failing, as there is a lack of accountability and proper scrutiny. Civil servants are not being held properly to account, whether this is for the implementation of taxes like IR35 or not enforcing tax collection on the large digital companies like Amazon and Google. Health and Education both have Ministers as they are considered essential parts of our well-being, tax is the same.

"HM Revenue & Customs is not directly accountable to the government. There is no minister with direct responsibility for taxation; nor is there a select committee on taxation in the House of Commons. These missing institutions leave tax administration without sufficient political over-sight and with too narrow a mandate, flaws compounded by an illusion that HMRC operates in an apolitical manner.

Under the present system in which HMRC feigns being apolitical and the Treasury manages the national budget in ways that in effect mean that tax functions as constraint on, rather than a facilitator of, social and economic policy. In addition, the absence of an Office for Tax Responsibility function is a serious shortcoming in Britain. To make the tax system democratically accountable parliament should allocate the resources to ensure effective monitoring of tax collection and its social and economic impact".(Richard Murphy)

So that: The tax function is accountable to Parliament and is more open and transparent.

How: The UK Border Agency was formerly a non-ministerial department, but due to issues of poor service it was brought back into the Home Office and Ministerial control.

A good way to remedy this and provide wider debate over the powers and actions of HMRC would be to have a Minister for HMRC. At present this responsibility is with one of the Treasury Team currently the Financial Secretary to the Treasury, but there isn't a clear line of responsibility and accountability.

Alternatively create a Ministry of Tax which is separate from the Treasury.

- Recommendation: Define a 4-year window for review of Freelancing policy and use of the FLC.

Why: We need to constantly review effectiveness around the issues of tax revenue; flexibility and prosperity add employment rights. To be considered on sectorial basis. This is good governance putting down a marker for review.

So that: As promised in the Labour Manifesto of 2017 (P51) : 'Labour recognises that the law often struggles to keep up with the ever-changing new forms of employment and work, so we will set up a dedicated commission to modernise the law around employment status. New statutory definitions of employment status would reduce the need for litigation and improve compliance. The commission will be led by legal and academic experts with representation from industry and trade unions'[vi].

How: Could add to governance structure of IR35 Forum

- **Recommendation: Revise the CEST tool for establishing employment status by sector and allow third parties to develop licensed tools using the business rules**

Why: We have established that indicators for self-employment don't necessarily follow a one size fits all approach. Any automated tool needs to take this into account.

So that: We have a tool based on business rules not just on software supplied centrally. Tools would still need to justify a position and a decision made.

How: CEST tool to use agreed precedents and cases and rules. To be agreed by the IR35 Forum as a governing body. The ability for third parties to develop tools which could be licensed \ approved should be considered. In IT terms any tool would need to pass a set of tests that is all. Indeed HMC could move to supply a set of open-api that could be used.

- **Recommendation: Suspend new IR35 roll-out to private sector and in public sector**

Do: In the immediate terms reset liability for IR35 assessment back to contractors. As the Chartered Institute of Taxation have suggested also strengthen the powers of HMRC to existing legislation. Suspend until at least 2021. We think that before making any significant changes in this area that the conclusion from RSA Matthew Taylor review need to be considered.

Why: Because we believe that the new rules are unnecessary, unfair and damaging to the self-employed, their clients and to the economy as a whole.

How: Depending on how entrenched the rules are in legislation, however it may be possible to modify the guidance around IR35.

- **Recommendation: Retain the IR35 forum, but with an independent chair**

Why: We think that the IR35 Forum has an important role to play but it needs to be more independent of HMRC and should be acting in more of a scrutiny than a consultation role.

How: We keep the Forum running as is, review partly its governance structure in the light of what we are doing with the FLC. However we should have the chairman elected from the Forum itself to build in some early accountability.

This is an idea also proposed by the economist Richard Murphy[vii].

Policy briefing for this was previously published. viii

- **Recommendation: Review role of Umbrella and payroll companies for employment rights and tax purposes and as vehicles that create bogus or forced self-employment. Encourage use of co-operatives.**

Why: Umbrella and payroll companies have a positive role to play, especially for those in the self-employment market for a short term. However, we need to guard against self-employed workers being rail-roaded into such schemes.

Currently rules forbid contractors forming a co-operative version of an Umbrella or payroll company (unless it is also done on a voluntary unpaid basis). In Belgium, SMART operates a very successful model along these lines. Labour should allow and support the creation of co-operatives in this area. Also allow contractors and self-employed to choose their preferred Umbrella company when it is appropriate to use on.

How: Consultation followed by any necessary legislative changes

Appendices

Recommendation: A Limited Liability model for freelancers

As taken from The Freelancing Agenda (2015). Further work on the idea was undertaken by IPSE and this should be referenced too.

An incoming government should consult on the introduction of a form of a limited liability company for a sole trader, or alternatively, a method of creating limited liability self-employment. It would consult on how this could interface with existing models, case law, and parallel legislation, such as rules for agency workers and those aimed at countering forced self-employment. The advantage of such an approach would be to create a vehicle for all legitimate freelancers to use. There are many possible ways forward and our recommendation is that change is made. We propose the establishment of a 'freelancer limited liability company' (FLC). This could follow the structure defined for Community-Interest-Companies (CIC). For

CIC's, a limited company is registered in the normal way but this is then registered as a CIC if it meets certain criteria. The legitimacy of this company would depend on meeting the requirements of the definition of freelancing outlined in section 2.1. A FLC company could work in a similar way and narrow the differentials between the self-employed model and the use of a limited company, such that the choice of model is driven by business or professional concerns rather than tax efficiencies. The criteria for registration could be a single shareholder who is the key income generator.

Once registered, it would identify the operator as a freelancer. They would be restricted from many of the abuses for tax avoidance as they wouldn't be able to have their spouses or others as shareholders. However, their status as a freelancer would be recognized and it would support the charter principles (ix) that they do not need to 'have concurrent clients or be able to supply a substitute, provide their own equipment, have a distinct work address or even grow their businesses, to prove their status as a freelancer'.

We would see the creation of a Freelancer Limited Liability company (FLC) as a vehicle to distinguish freelancers from the broader small business workforce. It could be used to limit tax avoidance and also be as a vehicle for tax credits, and to allow lower-paid freelance workers (precariat workers) to register for benefits and welfare support in between contracts. An FLC company would qualify to be able to use micro-accounting and so reduce much administrative burden. In the short term we would expect it to be a model for professional freelancers, but in the longer term as a vehicle to help freelance workers and the precariat workforce.

A FLC would offer more certainty over status for both tax and employment purposes. As it could still be a limited company, it would continue to interface with existing tax and employment law and regulations (such as Section 44 and other Agency workers directives).

By using this Freelancing Limited Liability Company (FLC) there would be the following advantages:

• No need to specify a substitute

• No need to have multiple or concurrent clients on the go

• Contracts under seven months automatically considered as genuine freelance

• The ability to register for benefits between contracts

• The improved ability to gain tax credits for sickness, maternity, paternity and other leave

• Limited liability status

• Simplified accounting

• Ability to pay expenses, including training, and carry monies over to future years

• Ability to employ other staff

• Right to comparison with other suppliers (See Charter iv)) The FLC would have the following limits:

• Single shareholder as the principal employee

• A fairly defined minimum salary/dividend split It is noted that any such structure would need to have a safeguards to prevent vulnerable workers from being forced into it.

References

[i] Worker status : https://www.gov.uk/employment-status/worker

[ii] https://www.contractorcalculator.co.uk/what_is_a_managed_service_company.aspx

[iii] https://www.contractoruk.com/news/0012197ipse_revives_freelancer_limited_company_plan.html

[iv] https://www.ftadviser.com/2015/07/08/ifa-industry/tax-planning/osborne-creates-dividend-allowance-Og1J5Dn3ahE7cjFMB8LnxJ/article.html

[v] https://www.bbc.co.uk/news/uk-england-nottinghamshire-33007103

[vi] Labour Manifesto 2017: https://labour.org.uk/wp-content/uploads/2017/10/labour-manifesto-2017.pdf

[vii] http://www.taxresearch.org.uk/Blog/2017/09/05/a-ministry-of-tax/

https://static1.squarespace.com/static/5991db18e4fcb5249
46fb639/t/59a886c88419c278e3035f2f/1504216779298/P
B_4+Ministry+of+Tax+Murphy+final.pdf

About the Author

Philip Ross is a Labour Party member and an Executive member of Labour Business Group and chairs their Freelancing policy pediment.

He has for a long time been an advocate of progressive small business policy in the Labour Party. In 2012, he re-launched the Labour Small Business Forum as a network of Labour members and supporters who work for themselves at well attended fringe meeting at the Labour Conference in Manchester, which he organised and chaired. The fledging group merged in with the Labour Business Group. He is also a member of SME4Labour.

In 1999, while working as a freelancer he helped to form the Professional Contractors Group(now known as IPSE), which is a trade association for freelancers. In 2012, he published his book 'Freedom to Freelance' that traces the formation of the group and their struggles to get all the political parties to understand the importance of freelancing and small business in the new economy.

In 2015 together with Professor Andrew Burke he co-authored the Labour Business policy booklet entitled 'The Freelancing Agenda'. He has subsequently worked with

Co-operatives(UK) as their ambassador on self-employment and was a co-author the 'Not Alone -trade union and co-operatives solutions for the self-employed'. He currently a leading advocate of WorkerTech.

Currently works as freelance business analyst trading through his own company, which is also a member of Sleuth Co-operative. He is also a non-executive member of Indycube – the co-operative for freelancers. Until last year he was also a Consultative Council member for IPSE.

He also sits on the Labour Party's Self-employment forum.

He is the former Mayor of Letchworth Garden City and a strong advocate of garden city principles for the social ownership of land and the city. He lives in Letchworth and is married with 3 children.

www.ingramcontent.com/pod-product-compliance
Lightning Source LLC
Chambersburg PA
CBHW060643210326
41520CB00010B/1717